SIGN HERE

a contracting boo

for children and their parents

SIGN HERE

a contracting book
for children and their parents

Jill C. Dardig
Russell Sage College

William L. Heward
The Ohio State University

Illustrations by
Ann Pearle

BEHAVIORDELIA
Kalamazoo, Michigan

International Standard Book Number:
  0-914-47419-7
Library of Congress Catalog Card:
  Summary: A family decides to try contingency
contracting in an attempt to improve parent-
child relations. Contains material for the reader
to use such as sample task and reward lists and
contracts.
  1. Children—Management—Juvenile literature.
[1. Parent and child. 2. Behavior. 3. Family life]
I. Heward, William L., 1949-   joint author.
II. Title.
HQ769.D23   301.42'7   76-18757

1 2 3 4 5 6 7 8 9
4 3 2 1 0 9 8 7 6

Printed and bound by:
Edwards Brothers
Ann Arbor, Michigan 48104

Those involved in the preparation of this book
were:

Designer: Mike Frazier
Illustrations by: Ann Pearle
Editors: Elizabeth L. C. Wolf
          Barbara E. Swart
Composition: Susan Wiltse
Mechanical preparation: Sharon Sattler

TABLE OF CONTENTS

ABOUT THE AUTHORS

Drs. Jill Dardig and William Heward bring their combined expertise in the field of psychology in education to this unique book.

Dr. Dardig is an Assistant Professor of Special Education at Russell Sage College where she teaches courses in special education, classroom management, and parent education. She has also served as Parent Educator at Project Change, an intensive day treatment program, in Massachusetts, for behaviorally disordered children; and as the Assistant Project Director of the Children's Video Theatre in Amherst, Massachusetts. In addition to her other activities, she has developed a wide variety of curriculum material for deaf children.

Dr. William Heward is an Assistant Professor with the Faculty for Exceptional Children at The Ohio State University. He is currently conducting research in special education technology, and teaching in the areas of behavior analysis and child management. He is also the past Director of Project Change and has written two other books, the *Teacher's Handbook for Use with the Visual Response System;* and, demonstrating his versatility, *Some Are Called Clowns: A Season with the Last of the Great Barnstorming Baseball Teams.*

PREFACE

While contingency contracting has been shown to be a powerful, yet simple means of solving many kinds of family problems, we do not view it as a cure-all. But perhaps it can be a beginning toward more appropriate human relationships. If nothing else, we hope that families will find contracting fun. And, if this book merely prompts people to sit down and listen to each other's concerns and desires, we will consider it a great success.

We have been fortunate throughout two years of conceptualizing, writing, field testing, and rewriting this book, to have received help from many friends and professional colleagues.

Jill would like to thank her mother, Evelyn Dardig, for encouraging and helping her with the original concept of a contracting book for children.

Bill would like to thank his colleagues at The Ohio State University, Drs. John O. Cooper, Thomas M. Stephens, and Raymond H. Swassing, for lending both professional and moral support to this writing effort.

Dr. Walter B. Barbe, on two separate occasions, read the entire manuscript and produced dozens of excellent suggestions and editorial changes which we incorporated into the book. Dr. Jon Stott, Associate Professor of English at the University of Alberta, also provided editorial assistance for which we are most grateful.

The best ideas are useless until someone provides a vehicle for their expression. We are grateful to the people at Behaviordelia for their belief in, and support of this project. Dick Malott and Don Whaley are to be praised for their pioneering behavior. Bonnie Clarke Wolf, our editor, is a true professional, and her tireless work is appreciated by us both.

The best thing that happened during the making of this book was when

Annie Pearle agreed to do the illustrations. She is a marvelous person to work with and an extremely talented artist.

Because of the efforts of two doctoral candidates in the Faculty for Exceptional Children at The Ohio State University, we were able to empirically validate the effectiveness of *Sign Here,* and to incorporate their research findings into the final version of the book. Mike Kabler used *Sign Here* to teach contracting skills to three classes of fourth grade students. Jim Norman gave copies of *Sign Here* to parents of behaviorally disordered children, and found the families were able to develop contracts which greatly reduced disruption in the home.

Pattie LeGendre and Beverly Smith could probably recite the book by heart. They typed the entire manuscript three times. Ida Halasz designed the Galen Official Seal, and Susan C. Quinn collected data from children on their preferences regarding artwork.

Most of all, we would like to express our gratitude to the more than 40 parents and 100 children who read early drafts of *Sign Here* and shaped our writing behavior with many pertinent comments. Their suggestions held top priority each time we reworked the manuscript.

Again, we do not view contingency contracting as a cure-all. But we do see it as a step in the direction of more appropriate human relationships. And, as we said at the outset, if *Sign Here* merely prompts people to sit down and listen to each other's concerns and desires, we will consider it a great success.

J.C.D. and W.L.H.
Columbus, Ohio
June, 1976

FOREWORD

Sign Here is a book for children, parents, and teachers. It is, first of all, a children's story involving the problems with a family as the different members learn how to live together cooperatively and happily. The variety of characters, without the emphasis being placed upon any one member, makes identification with a character especially easy. Their problems are not unusual and, as such, are ones with which any member of a family can readily identify.

The story has all of the necessary elements: Early presentation of a problem, so important if reader interest is going to be maintained; followed by sufficient character development so that the reader knows the people and can identify with some one of the characters; development of the plot as an attempt is made to solve the problems; and a convincing conclusion as the problem is resolved.

The theme presented is significant — the relationships between children and their parents. Interestingly, the authors have succeeded in building a relationship between the children and their parents, between the parents themselves and among the children within the family. But the manner of the resolution of the family problems is the unique contribution of this story.

The authors present a plan called "contracting", which, unfortunately, is better known among professional family workers than among parents. And since the only hope for the procedure to work is within the family itself, it is in the translation of the concepts of contracting into the child-parent family relationship that the authors have made the greatest contribution.

The title of the book, *Sign Here*, suggests both the solution of the story itself and the suggestion to the reader that this may be an approach well worth trying. Essentially, the procedure is to enter into a contract (hence the title, *Sign Here*) to perform certain duties or behave in a particular manner. But *Sign Here* does not end with just the suggestion that a family try out "contracting." Direct involvement of the reader is made easy by the inclusion of a Do-It-Yourself Contracting Kit, presenting a step-by-step procedure for solving interfamily relationship conflicts, from an initial family conference through the procedures of choosing a task and a reward for its successful completion, drawing up the contract, and fulfilling the contract. The kit contains numerous examples of the types of problems which frequently arise within a family and suggested contracts which might be applicable. Tear-out forms are also provided.

Sign Here can become a significant contribution to family living. In the ever increasingly complex society in which children are being reared, approaches which recognize the contribution of every member of the family to the happiness of the family unit are most welcome. Contracting is an effective yet simple means for families to solve many of their problems — *Sign Here* tells how.

Walter B. Barbe, Editor
Highlights for Children

SIGN HERE

a contracting book

for children and their parents

EDITOR'S NOTE

One of the subtle areas of sexual discrimination has been nurtured by certain rules of language usage, and the desire to maintain a stylistic flow in literary works. This phenomenon occurs regularly in the rule that calls for the agreement in number between antecedent nouns and their pronouns, i.e., "*everyone* must tie *his* (not *their*) shoes," the singular "one" calling for the singular "his" or "her." The discriminatory factor has occurred, until recently, in the universal use of the pronoun "his," in that position. To avoid this situation, solutions ranging from the use of "his/her," "his or her," "s/he," to the use of the neuter "ne," have been employed. However, they contribute a disconcerting ungainliness to many sentences, especially where the need for agreement occurs in more than one instance in a given sentence.

The American Psychological Association has suggested, in a recent position paper, that psychologists and students of psychology, in the interest of neutrality, and lack of complexity, adopt the plural form following the singular antecedent, i.e., "everyone has to tie *their* shoes." In support of this position, we have, in this text, adhered to the suggestion and employed the use of plural pronouns.

In preparing our manuscripts for publication, our editorial style guides for capitalization, punctuation, and grammar are the *Publication Manual of the American Psychological Association*, and *A Manual of Style*, The University of Chicago Press.

A SHORT FLIGHT

The two boys bounded through the house. They threw open the door to Jeff's bedroom and flopped on the floor.

"Wow, we musta just made a world record," Perry said, trying to catch his breath.

"That's the most I've ever run without stopping once," Jeff agreed. He got up off the floor. "C'mon, don't you remember why we ran all the way?"

"Okay, okay Jeff." Perry opened the box he had with him. "Here it is."

"Can I hold it?" Jeff asked.

"Sure, you can even fly it when we get outside."

Jeff moved his fingers all over the model airplane. It was beautiful. Jeffrey Galen loved planes. The walls of his room were covered with pictures of them. And though he'd put together lots of plastic model airplanes, he'd never had one that could really fly.

"Let's go," he shouted. The two boys ran through the house, knocking over a kitchen chair as they hurried to get outside.

"We can fly it in the backyard," Jeff said.

The airplane had a tiny engine, no bigger than his thumb. He wondered how it could ever fly. But when Perry started it, the propellor spun so fast, Jeff couldn't even see it. *This* plane would fly. And fly it did. In a few seconds Perry had the little blue model buzzing around and around in circles high above their heads. The engine which had looked so small sure didn't sound small. You could hear the *Whirr-Whirr* for two blocks!

"Here Jeff, you try it."

"Sure," Jeff said. But before Perry could hand him the controls, the fun ended.

"Hey, what are you two kids doing out there? I never heard so much noise in all my life!"

It was Jeff's father yelling from his bedroom window. "Turn that motor off before I come down there and wrap that plane around a tree. Perry, you'd better go home now. Jeffrey, get in the house. And wipe your feet. You're always tracking mud all over the kitchen floor."

2

Jeff said goodbye to Perry. All of a sudden the great day was turning bad. Jeff walked into the house with his head down and mumbled a weak hello to his older sister Lynn.

Well, at least he wouldn't be the only one in trouble tonight. His mother would be home from work soon, and Lynn was supposed to get dinner started instead of talking on the telephone. And he was getting pretty hungry now too.

Jeff found his father in the bathroom shaving. "Sorry dad," he said as he watched his sleepy father pull the razor across his soapy face. "We didn't mean to wake you up. It just seems funny to me that somebody would be sleeping in the middle of the day. I always forget."

"Well, we're going to have to do something about your memory then, aren't we? Look son, some people are lucky enough to work in the daytime. Me, I work at night. That means I've got to get some sleep during the day. I don't like it any better than you kids do."

Jeff thought about how tired and dirty his father looked when he came

home each morning just when the rest of the family was getting ready to start the day.

"I know you've got to get your rest, dad. I'll try not to let it happen again."

"Being sorry isn't enough. You've been saying that all along. This must be the fifth time in the last two weeks you woke me up when you came home from school. We've got to do something about this."

Jeff really was sorry he'd bothered his dad. But it hurt him that his father griped at him all the time. He really *did* forget he was sleeping.

Just then Jeff's mother came home from work. He knew she was home because he could hear her yelling at Lynn.

"Hi mom," he said as he popped into the kitchen. His little sister Pamela was there too.

"Try to catch me," she shouted, and Jeff began chasing her around the room. She giggled and laughed out loud as she ran.

"Jeffrey, stop chasing Pamela around the house!" his mother yelled.

"Stop it this instant! You haven't even fed the dog or taken out the trash today."

"Wow, what is this?" Jeff whined. "The day for everyone to jump on me?"

"Not only that, he and one of his friends woke me up again," Jeff's dad added as he entered the kitchen.

"Jeffrey, what *are* we going to *do* with you?" his mother asked. "And Lynn, will you get off the telephone and help get supper started? *Pamela,* what are you doing to that poor dog? Stop that!"

"Don't holler at Pam like that. She's just a baby," his father shouted.

Woof-woof-woof. Now it was the dog's turn. Rags was behind the wastebasket barking and yelping at the fighting people. Jeff reached down and tucked the dog under his arm. He grabbed the wastebasket with his other hand and ran out of the house. He put Rags down on the grass and emptied the wastebasket into the trash can.

"Can you believe this family? Fight, fight, fight. Nag, nag, nag. I bet I get yelled at for something every day."

Rags was sitting at Jeff's feet wagging his tail and looking up at the boy's face. Jeff picked up a stick and gave it a long toss. Rags ran after it. He clutched the stick in his teeth and ran back to Jeff. The boy threw it again.

Jeff loved his parents and sisters. In fact, he was sure they all loved each other.

"I just don't know why we fight so much," he said as he took the stick from the dog's mouth. "When things are like this at home, I wish I were someplace else. Even at school taking an arithmetic test." Jeff threw the stick with all his might.

At least he knew he wasn't alone. Lots of his friends said everyone yelled at each other at their houses too.

But then Jeff thought of all the good times his family had together. Why did they ever have to fight at all?

Jeffrey and Rags played together in the backyard until Lynn called them in for supper. Things didn't get any better during dinner. Everyone

complained about everyone else.

"Jeffrey, you never pick up any of your things. Do you think we can go around picking up after you all the time?"

"Lynn, you spend half your life on that phone."

"Mom and dad, you two are always yelling at us. Do this. Do that."

Finally, Evelyn Galen slammed her hands down on the table. Everyone stopped talking.

"All right," she said. "That's enough! No more arguing! We're all part of this family and we have to work things out together. Let's just be quiet for the rest of the meal. *All* of us. After supper we're going to clear the table and have a family meeting. It's time we made some changes around here."

THE MEETING 2

"All right everyone, this meeting of the Galen family will now come to order. It's time we did something about all the fighting going on around here. If you kids would just do what you're supposed to do, it would be much more peaceful and happy in this house."

Jeff tried to look away as his father stared at him. "Jeff, isn't there any way we can get you to be quiet when you come home from school? You know I work all night long while the rest of you are sleeping."

"I try hard, dad, but after school all day I've just got to have some fun."

"You have your fun all right, and the few jobs you have to do don't get done. Your mother gets home from work and the garbage is still in the house, Rags hasn't been fed and watered, your room's a mess and on and on and on. What are we going to do with you?"

"Jeff's not the only one who doesn't do his share around here," Jeff's mother added. "Lynn, it seems like every day when I get home from work you're gabbing on the phone with one of your friends. You know how much we need your help."

"But mom," Lynn pleaded, "if I work really hard and get dinner started before you get home, you still yell at me for being on the phone."

All at once Jeff's mother jumped up from the table. "Pamela no!" she shouted. "Get away from that fish bowl. How many times have I told you not to put your hands in the water?"

Jeff didn't even have to look. He knew his little sister was playing one of her favorite games — trying to catch the goldfish. Evelyn Galen pulled her daughter away from the fish bowl. Then she picked it up and set it on the top shelf of the bookcase.

"What are we going to do with you kids? You're driving us crazy. Can't we ever have any peace and quiet around here?"

"Well, how about you?" Lynn asked. "You two are always shouting at us for something. It seems like we can't do anything right."

"All right, all right," her mother said. "Enough arguing. Everyone here has complaints. No one is perfect. We have to work out something that's good for all of us. We're a family, and we all love each other, don't we?"

"Yes mom," Jeff agreed.

"You're right, honey," Joseph Galen added.

"I love you mommy and daddy," Pamela said, running over to hug her parents.

"I've got an idea that maybe we could try," Lynn offered.

"What is it?" everyone asked.

"Well, it sounds funny, I mean for a family to do it. But we do it in Ms. Johnson's English class and it works great."

"Do what?" her father asked. "If you think you have an idea that'll help, tell us what it is."

"Okay. Just remember I told you it would sound strange."

"Tell us."

"Well, in English class we all make *contracts* with Ms. Johnson for the jobs, or *tasks*, we have to do."

"Contracts? What could contracts have to do with our family?" Lynn's mother wanted to know.

"What's a contract?" Jeff asked.

"A contract is an agreement. It says what you must do and also what you'll get in return for doing it. Then every time you finish the task on your contract you get to do something you like. I think the good thing about contracts is that everyone has to agree to everything in them."

"So you think we could have contracts with each other in the family?" Lynn's father asked.

"I told you you'd think it was a dumb idea."

"I didn't say it was dumb. I just don't see why you need a contract to do what you're supposed to do anyway. Your mother and I never had contracts with our parents. But the way things have been going around here, I'm willing to try anything."

"Maybe contracts are just what we need," his wife said. "Especially if they would get you kids to obey us."

"But contracts also say what you and dad have to do. There's got to be a *reward* for meeting our contracts," Lynn said.

"What's with all this reward stuff?" her father asked. "That bothers me. You kids should be good without getting paid off. It's just like bribing your own kids to do what they should do anyway."

"Wait honey, we like to do fun things with the children anyway. But with a contract they'd just have to earn special privileges, that's all. It might make them more responsible and cut down some of the fighting that goes on around here."

"Well, I never said I wouldn't give it a try," he answered.

"Really! Can we try it?" Lynn asked.

"What does a contract look like?" Jeff asked his sister.

"Contracts are written on a piece of paper, Jeffrey. When two people make a contract with each other they both agree to everything the contract tells them to do."

"But what makes them do it? How can a piece of paper make anybody do anything?"

"Remember what I said before?" Lynn answered. "When you finish the task on the contract, you get the reward on the contract. In English class, each time I finish ten pages in my workbook, I get to read anything I want for ten minutes. I can even bring my favorite magazine to school. But, before you sign a contract, you agree to *everything* it says. Contracts have to be *fair* for everyone."

"So I wouldn't write my name on a contract if I didn't think it was fair. Is that what you mean?"

"Yes. That's exactly right. There's also one more thing that helps make contracts work."

"What's that?"

"An official seal."

"An official seal?" Jeff asked.

"Yes. The seal is a little drawing or picture at the bottom of the contract that shows it's official and you must live up to it."

"Well, mom and dad," Lynn asked, "what do you think about us making contracts with you for the things we're supposed to do?"

"We're willing to give it a try," her parents replied together.

"I thought since it was my idea, I'd offer to have the first contract to see if it works," Lynn said.

"I want a contract, too," Jeff burst out.

"Okay," his father said. "There's no reason why you each can't have a contract of your own."

"Mine will be about helping get supper ready," Lynn said.

"Mine will be for not waking up dad when I get home from school," Jeff shouted.

"Why don't we all think about what we want our contracts to say," his mother said. "Tomorrow night we can make them up."

"And I'm going to make an official seal to put on all our contracts to help make them work," Jeff added, and he hurried off to his room.

Jeff gathered everything he would need to make the Galen Official Seal and sat down at his desk. "Let's see, I've got paints, brushes, paper, and scissors. That should do it." Then he started to draw. He had lots of ideas.

"Too dull . . . Too jumbled up . . . Not exactly . . . There, that's it!"

And he set to work on a perfect copy. In half an hour he was finished and sat back to admire his work.

JEFF'S CONTRACT

3

The next morning Jeff invited everyone into his room to see the Galen Official Seal. He had taped it to the wall and covered it with a white handkerchief. While they all watched, Jeff pulled away the cloth like a magician.

"Not bad," his father said.

"It's beautiful Jeff," his mother smiled.

"Now *that's* an Official Seal!" Lynn agreed.

"Juice," Pamela cooed. She had spied an open jar of bright orange paint and was heading for it. Lynn turned in time to see where her little sister was going and reached out to stop her . . . Too late! . . . Splat!!! The paint splashed all over the smooth wood floor. It looked like a million ladybugs doing a mixed-up square dance.

"Oh, no! What a mess! It'll take an hour to clean it up," Jeff's father moaned. "And look at the rest of this room. I'll bet you haven't put anything away since your eighth birthday."

"Well," Jeff looked around his room. He had to admit . . . *Nobody* would call it neat. "I know. How about making *that* my first contract?

Cleaning up my room I mean?"

"We'd better try something," his mother said. "Looks like a bomb went off in here."

"Get a piece of paper Jeff, and I'll show you how we can write up your first contract," Lynn offered.

Somehow Jeff found a pencil and a large piece of paper in the mess on his desk. "Now we're ready," Lynn said. "On the left side of the contract you write what job or task you're supposed to do. On the right side you write the reward you'll get for doing the task. Jeff, then you and mom or dad will sign the contract and put on the seal. That's all there is to it."

"Okay," Jeff said. He quickly wrote "Clean up bedroom" on one side of the contract. "Mom, dad, what do you think we should put as the reward?"

"Well, Jeffrey, I have an idea," his father said. "Your mother and I pick up after you kids all the time. If you stick to this contract, it would sure make life a lot easier for us. So how about this for a reward? If you clean up your room for a whole week, I'll spend two hours of special time with you on Saturday. Just you and me. We can play ball, paint, ride bikes, work on a model together, whatever you want. How about that?"

"Sounds super, dad!"

On the other side of the paper Jeff's father wrote: "Time with dad on Saturday." Then he taped the Galen Official Seal on the contract. And they both signed it at the bottom.

"It's done," Jeff said happily.

"Well, the contract's written son, but your room is still a disgrace. And you'll be late for school if we stick around here talking about this any longer. Tell you what. I'll help you get this paint wiped up. Then you'd better take off. You can clean up the rest when you get home."

They found some old rags and paint thinner and soon had the floor looking like new. "Gotta run now, dad."

"I'll say you'd better run. And make sure you put those dirty rags in the trash can so they don't start a fire. I'm going to bed."

Jeff ran all the way to school. Four blocks without stopping. Maybe these contracts would make things better at home. It felt good to run.

LOOPHOLES

4

Jeff ran all the way home from school, too. He wanted to get a head start on doing his contract. But he slowed down when he reached the house. He didn't want to wake up his father again.

And doing his contract was really easy. He put his paints, toys, and models back on the shelf, made his bed, and put away his clothes. "Nothing to it," he thought. Then he looked over his whole room. He had to admit his room *did* look pretty good when it was neat. Jeff felt very proud as he washed up for supper.

As soon as the Galens finished dinner, Jeff grabbed his father by the arm. "C'mon dad, let's check my contract."

"Okay, okay, I'm coming," and he followed his son into the bedroom.

Jeff was excited. "Well, how'd I do, dad?" he asked.

"Sorry son. Your desk is still a mess. Guess you don't make the contract today."

"But dad, you didn't say anything about my desk being neat, too. Gee, the rest of the room looks great. I lived up to my part of the contract."

"As far as I'm concerned, you didn't," his father replied.

Lynn was curled up around a big pillow on the living room floor. She looked up from her book. She could hear the argument coming from her brother's room. "Uh-oh," she thought. She hopped up and went into Jeff's room. "Maybe I can help straighten this out," she offered.

"It's no use. These contracts of yours just don't work."

"I'm afraid your brother's right, Lynn," her father added. "We went through a big deal making a contract with Jeffrey, and he still didn't clean up his room."

"I did too clean it up. What a rip-off!" Jeff cried.

"Now wait a second," Lynn said. "I think the contract will still work. It's just that I forgot to mention the most important rule about making contracts. You have to be *specific*."

"What does 'pacific' mean?"

"It means you have to say exactly what the task is right on the contract. And it's not 'Pacific' like the ocean, it's *specific*. Then no one can argue later

about whether or not they completed the task. And that's the problem here."

"Oh, how do you know all this stuff?" Jeff asked. "You always think you're so smart."

"No, it's not that, Jeff. I told my teacher we were going to try contracts at home and she let me borrow this book." Lynn handed Jeff and her dad a small book. "She said we could use it to help set up our contracts. It's even got some forms to write contracts on. We had the same problem at school with our contracts. At first we weren't specific enough and they didn't work."

Lynn showed her brother and father some of the contracts in the book. They looked at examples of good ones and bad ones.

"Here Jeff, let's tear out one of the blank contract forms from this book and write your contract again. After the part that says How Well you're supposed to do the task, let's be *specific* about cleaning your room."

"I get it," Jeff said. "I'll just list all the things I'm supposed to do in my room each day!" He made a list on the new contract form.

34

1. Pick up all clothes off floor, bed, desk, and chair.

2. Put all toys, models, and painting things on shelves.

3. Clear off desk top and straighten papers, books, and pencils.

4. Make bed.

"Okay, dad, how's this?"

"Looks fine Jeffrey. Let's try the contract again tomorrow."

"But dad, what if I miss just one day? Does that mean we have to miss out on Saturday?"

"I see what you mean. No one's perfect. We'll add that you can miss one day a week and still get your reward. But just one day — no more!"

"There's just one more thing dad," Lynn said as they started to sign the new contract.

"What's that?"

"If you're making Jeff be specific about the task, then you must be the same way about the reward. Remember, contracts have to be *fair* and *clear* for both people."

CONTRACT

TASK

Who: Jeffrey Galen

What: Clean up bedroom

When: ROOM EACH NIGHT AFTER SUPPER
Every day — DAD WILL CHECK

How Well: floor, bed, desk, and chair.
1. Pick up all clothes off
2. Put all toys, models, and painting
things on shelves.   3. Clear off desk top
and straighten papers, books, and pencils.
4. Make bed.   Jeff can miss 1 day a
week and still get reward.

Sign Here: _Jeffrey Galen_

Sign Here: _Joseph W. Galen_

REWARD

Who: DAD

What: TIME WITH DAD

When: on SATURDAY
2 HOURS, JUST JEFF

How Much: AND DAD, AT JEFF'S
CHOICE OF THE FOLLOWING: PLAYING
BALL, BIKE RIDING, PAINTING, WORKING
ON A MODEL, TRIP TO THE ZOO.
JEFF CAN BRING A FRIEND ALONG
iF HE WANTS.

Date: March 30

Date: March 30

IN THIS FAMILY WE TRUST — G

TASK RECORD

"You're right, Lynn. All right Jeff, bring that contract here one more time and we'll fix up the other half." Under "Time with dad on Saturday," Jeff's father wrote: "Two hours of time, just Jeff and dad, doing Jeff's choice of the following: Playing ball, bike riding, painting, working on a model."

"Put down going to the zoo, too," Jeff pleaded.

"Okay." Joseph Galen added "trip to the zoo" to the contract.

"And can I bring a friend along if I want to?"

"Sure." And he added that Jeff could bring a friend. "Now I'll check your room each night this week after supper." And he wrote "Check room each night after supper" on the contract.

"Good, and I'm going to look at the contract so I know just what I have to do each day," Jeff said.

* * *

Jeff went straight to his room when he got home from school the next day. He picked up his contract and looked at the things he had to do.

"Hhhmmm, I wonder if that's what it *really* means?" he thought as he read the first part of the task. It read, "Pick up all clothes off floor, bed, desk, and chair." Jeff went ahead to the other parts of his task and finished them. He put all his toys, models, books, and painting things away. He cleared off his desk, straightened his papers, and made his bed.

Then he looked at the first part again. "Pick up all clothes off floor, bed, desk, and chair."

"Okay, that's what it says, and that's what I'm going to do."

Jeff laughed as he gathered up his clothes lying around the room. Then he got some more clothes from the closet. He would need a lot of clothes to test this contract. When he finished, everything looked just the way he wanted it to. He closed the door to his room and went outside to play. After supper he'd *really* find out if contracts worked.

That night, Jeff's whole family followed him to his room to check his contract. They thought he'd acted a little funny during supper, but they didn't know why until he threw open the door.

"What do you think, everybody?"

Lynn and her mother started to laugh. Joseph Galen couldn't believe his eyes for a few seconds, but then he started laughing, too. Even little Pamela enjoyed the scene.

"Look mommy, Jeffie's pants are all up in the sky."

"Well, did I make my contract dad?"

"You must be kidding!"

"Wait honey, Jeffrey did do what the contract said. He picked up all of his clothes off the floor, the bed, the chair, and the desk," his mother said.

"He sure did!"

Two of Jeff's shirts dangled from the lamp. Socks and underwear covered several planes hanging from the ceiling. And a pair of blue jeans was draped over the picture on the wall.

"What a loophole!" his father laughed.

"What dad?"

"Oh, nothing son. Okay, I guess I've got to give you a check mark for

CONTRACT

TASK

Who: Jeffrey Galen

What: Clean up bedroom

When: Every day – DAD WILL CHECK
ROOM EACH NIGHT AFTER SUPPER
1. Pick up all clothes off

How Well: floor, bed, desk, and chair.
2. Put all toys, models, and painting
things on shelves. 3. Clear off desk top
and straighten papers, books, and pencils.
4. Make bed. Jeff can miss 1 day a
week and still get reward.

All clothes must be put away
or hung up in closet. G. B. J. N. G.

REWARD

Who: DAD

What: Time with DAD

When: on SATURDAY
2 HOURS, JUST JEFF

How Much: AND DAD, AT JEFF'S
CHOICE OF THE FOLLOWING : PLAYING
BALL, BIKE RIDING, PAINTING, WORKING
ON A MODEL, TRIP TO THE ZOO.
JEFF CAN BRING A FRIEND ALONG
IF HE WANTS.

Sign Here: Jeffrey Galen   Date: March 30

Sign Here: Joseph N. Galen   Date: March 30

TASK RECORD

M	T	W	Th	F	S	Su	M	T	W	Th	F	S	Su	M
JWG														

meeting your contract today. I want to show you I'm going to be honest about these contracts. You did what it says, so you get the reward. But what do you say we make a little change on your contract to cover this pants in the sky trick?"

"Sure dad. I was just having some fun. Testing you and mom to see if you really meant this contract stuff. Here, I'll write it in."

Jeff took a pen and added "All clothes must be put away in drawers or hung up in closet." He and his dad put their initials next to the change to show they agreed with it.

The next night when Joseph Galen checked his son's room it was neat and clean just like the contract said. "Looks great Jeff," he said to his son who waited proudly at the door to his bedroom.

"Thanks dad." Jeff thought of the fun they would have on Saturday. He was glad his father seemed in such a good mood, and he made a promise to himself to try extra hard to be quiet when he came home from school.

CONTRACT

TASK

Who: _Lynn Shler_

What: _Help prepare supper_

When: _Mon.—Fri., by 5:00 p.m._

How Well: Help prepare supper. _Mom or dad will leave a list of what to fix._

Sign Here: ➡ _Lynn Shler_

Sign Here: ➡ _Evelyn Shler_

REWARD

Who: _Mom_

What: _Phone calls for Lynn_

When: _Every night_

How Much: Privacy for Lynn to _make phone calls for 30 minutes after supper. Can call Sat. and Sun. if she made contract the rest of the week._

Date: _April 1_

Date: _April 1_

IN THIS FAMILY WE TRUST G ★

TASK RECORD

LYNN GETS A PRIVATE LINE   5

When Lynn's mother walked through the front door she was greeted by the sound of her daughter laughing and talking on the telephone. "Well," she thought, "maybe Lynn has started supper already." She took a deep breath. Could she smell anything cooking? No. Nothing.

Lynn hung up the phone quickly as her mother came into the kitchen.

"Okay Lynn, I think it's time we worked out your first contract. You can probably guess what it will be about."

"Sure can, mom," Lynn said. "I've got some more contract forms in my room. I'll go draw one up."

Lynn was back in the kitchen five minutes later, handing her mother the new contract. A copy of the Galen Official Seal was taped to the bottom.

"How does it sound?" she asked after her mother had read the contract.

"It sounds just fine, Lynn. After we sign it, let's tape it here on the cabinet door to remind both of us."

Lynn arrived home at four thirty the next afternoon and headed right for the kitchen and her chores. By five o'clock she had chicken frying in a

heavy pan. She began cutting tomatoes for a salad and putting them into a large glass bowl. She looked up from the food as her mother came into the kitchen.

"Lynn, how nice. It looks like dinner's almost ready."

"Thanks, mom. How was your day?"

"Fine, dear. Now why don't you get a head start on your homework. I'll take over the salad and cook some rice. You can wake up your father now, too. I'll call you when supper's ready."

At seven o'clock, dinner was over and they'd finished the dishes. Jeff and his parents gathered around the TV for a special nature program. Lynn was alone in the kitchen chatting on the phone with her friend Karen. Pamela was playing with her building blocks. It seemed to her family that no two of Pam's creations were ever alike. Her building blocks were all different sizes. Some were very big and some very small. She would pile the big blocks up high, then climb up on top of them.

Joseph Galen looked over at his daughter. "Pamela, that's a beautiful

building. You're really good at building with those blocks," he said.

Pamela smiled and went on playing.

It was eight o'clock when Lynn's mother looked at her watch.

"Oh no! We've been so interested in this show, we didn't notice that Lynn's been on the phone for a whole hour. And our contract said just thirty minutes. I'm going to put a stop to this right now!"

Just then, Lynn appeared at the door.

"Uhh, I guess I was on the phone too long, huh?"

"Yes Lynn, you know you were. I just don't think it's fair for you to take advantage of your contract like that."

"But mom, I didn't do it on purpose. I just get started talking and the time flies by. I didn't know I was on the phone that long, honest."

Jeff jumped up from the couch. "Hey, I have an idea. Follow me."

Lynn and her parents followed Jeff into the kitchen. He stopped in front of the stove.

"Here's the answer," he said, and pointed to the back of the stove.

"Oh, the oven timer. Why didn't I think of that? I'll just set it for thirty minutes when I start my call and hang up when the buzzer goes off."

"That's a good idea, Jeff," his mother said. "Lynn, let's give your contract another try tomorrow."

"Now," Jeff said with a grin, "as long as everyone's here, let's make some popcorn."

They all agreed it was a great idea. Within minutes kernels of popcorn were hopping madly in the pan.

Pop-pop-pop-*Splash*-pop-pop!

"Did you hear that splash?" Lynn asked slowly.

"Why yes."

Another loud *Splash* echoed in the kitchen.

"Uh oh, you don't think . . ." Jeff's dad darted toward the living room.

PAMELA THE PET MENACE 6

Everyone arrived in the living room just in time to see little Pam getting ready to drop another one of her building blocks into the goldfish bowl. "Stop that, Pamela!" her mother shouted. The little girl whirled around and dropped the block to the floor next to the makeshift ladder she was standing on.

Pamela had found a way to stack her blocks so she could climb up on them and reach the goldfish. She would perch on top of her homemade ladder, and bomb the little yellow animals by dropping small blocks into their bowl. Lynn lifted her sister down.

"Poor fish," Jeff sighed as he pulled out two blocks from the bottom of the bowl. "At least they can still swim."

Suddenly Jeff remembered the popcorn. He couldn't hear the rat-a-tat-tat sound of bursting kernels anymore. He ran into the kitchen and pulled the pan off the stove just as it began to smoke.

"Whew, that was close!" he thought. He poured the popcorn into a big bowl, grabbed some napkins and salt, and carried everything into

the living room.

Pamela headed for the big bowl of warm popcorn while her father took apart her homemade ladder.

"I wish there was something we could do about the way she treats the pets," her mother said.

"I do, too," Lynn agreed. "Pamela, if you're not trying to catch the goldfish, you're pulling on Rags' tail or pinching his ears."

Pam didn't pay any attention to what they were saying. She just kept stuffing popcorn into her mouth. She looked like she was trying to set a world record for the most kernels of popcorn a three-and-a-half-year-old could stuff into her mouth.

"Well, I know one way of ending this problem real quick," her father suggested. "We can just get rid of the dog and those fish. That'll solve it."

"Daddy!" Jeff and Lynn wailed.

Evelyn Galen sided with the children. "Joseph, you know how important it is for Pam to learn how to respect and love animals."

"I agree with you, Evelyn. But we spend half our time yelling at her about the pets. And worst of all, it doesn't do any good. The more we yell, the more she hurts them. Nothing seems to work."

"I know!" Jeff shouted. Everyone stopped talking and looked at him. Even Pamela stopped reaching for more popcorn. "Let's all have a contract with Pam about Rags and the fish."

Lynn started laughing. "Jeffrey, don't you remember? A contract is a written agreement. Pam's only three-and-a-half years old. She doesn't read or write. How could she understand a contract?"

"But who said a contract has to be written in *words*?" Jeff replied.

"What?" everyone asked at once.

"We'll use pictures," Jeff went on. "We can cut out pictures and make drawings for the things in her contract. Then we'll explain it to her and tape it to the goldfish bowl to remind her."

"Hey! That just might work!"

"I want a contack, too," Pamela hollered between mouthfuls of popcorn.

"Then it's settled," her parents said. "We'll give it a try. Let's all get to work on Pam's contract."

Jeff's mother went to the closet and pulled down a large stack of old magazines she'd been saving for the Scouts' paper drive.

"We should be able to find some good pictures in these."

All of the Galens started looking through the magazines except Pam. She was still eating popcorn. Before long they found a picture of a boy and girl playing happily with a dog.

"That one should be perfect," Jeff said and ran to his room to get a pair of scissors. When he came back he had a piece of red construction paper, tape, and crayons, too. He cut out the dog picture and taped it to the left side of the construction paper.

"I'll draw some fish next to it," he said. And he drew a picture of two goldfish in a bowl. He put big smiles on their faces to show they were very happy.

"That looks really good, son," his father said. "Those pictures should help Pam remember to play nicely with Rags and to leave the fish alone. That's her part of the contract. Now, what are we going to put on the right side of the paper to stand for Pamela's reward for doing her part?"

He didn't wonder for long. Pamela came over to the stack of magazines just as her father had finished talking. She picked up one and held it out to her sister. "Read me a story, Lynn. Read me a story."

Everyone laughed. They could all see what her reward should be. One of her favorite things was to have someone read her a story from one of her books. Lynn looked through the magazines until she found a picture of some books. She cut it out and taped it to the contract. Then Jeff added the Galen Official Seal. The piece of red construction paper was now an official contract.

"Here's your contract, Pam," Jeff said. His little sister clutched at the red paper and smiled. Then her mother took her hand and pointed to each part of the contract and explained what it meant. If Pamela would play nicely with Rags — not hit him or pull his ears or tail — and just look at the fish without touching them, then Lynn or Jeffrey or one of her parents would read her a story before she went to bed. And she had to be good to the animals from the time she got home each afternoon until her bedtime to earn her reward.

"I like that, mommy," she said. "I'll be good to Rags and the fish."

Lynn and Jeff and their parents signed the bottom of the contract. Jeff handed the pen to his little sister, and she made a funny looking squiggle mark on the red paper.

"There, Pamela, now you have an Official Galen Contract!"

"Contack! Contack!" she yelled, and she jumped up and down happily.

Then Jeff showed Pamela he was taping the contract to the fish bowl so it would remind her to be good to the pets.

* * *

The next afternoon when Pamela came home from the day care center, she went straight for the fish bowl. Her mother held her breath as Pam reached out for the fish. But the little girl just pointed to the red paper

hanging there and said, "Contack!"

Her mother sighed with relief. Pamela had remembered her contract. She played with her building blocks until supper was ready and didn't go near the fish again.

Pam went over and sat by the fish bowl when dinner was over. She just stared at the two shiny fish darting around in the clear water. She was being good though, and kept her hands in her lap. She looked over to see what her family would do because she was sitting so close to the fish. Everyone seemed to be ignoring her. She moved closer to the bowl. Still no one paid any attention to her like they usually did. She moved still closer to the fish . . . so close that her nose almost squashed against the cold glass. Everyone acted like she wasn't even there. She waited a little longer. Then, she let out a little yelp and shot one of her hands into the fish bowl, making a big splash.

"Pamela, no!" everyone shouted, and rushed over to pull her away from the fish.

"I knew it was just too good to be true," her mother said. "Just when I thought it might really work."

"Me too," her father added. "I guess Lynn was right. Pam is just too young to understand a contract. We'll have to forget it. I'll take the fish back to the pet store tomorrow."

"No, wait," Lynn pleaded. "I think Pamela does understand her contract. It's the rest of us that don't understand."

"What do you mean?" Jeff asked.

"Well, a contract is an agreement that says if you do something, then something good will happen to you. You'll get a reward. That makes you keep wanting to do that task again. Right?"

Her family nodded in agreement.

"Okay, Pam did what she was supposed to do. She didn't bother the fish or hurt Rags for over two hours, but nothing good happened. We just ignored her. Just a minute. I'll be right back." Lynn hurried off toward her bedroom.

"But nothing was *supposed* to happen," Jeff yelled after her. "The contract said Pam couldn't bother the pets all evening. *Then* she would get her story."

"That's just what I mean, Jeffrey. That's our problem," Lynn said. She was carrying the contract book her teacher had given her.

"You don't have to say any more, Lynn. I see now what you're trying to tell us. I should have thought of it myself," her mother said. "One whole evening is just too long for a three-and-a-half-year-old. It must seem like years to her. Pamela was being perfectly good, but we all ignored her."

"And the only way she could get us to pay attention was to reach into the goldfish bowl," Jeff added.

"Now you've got what I mean," Lynn said. "I think our contract with Pam will work. We just have to make it for smaller amounts of time. See what it says here?"

Lynn showed her parents and brother a part of the contracting book. It told about the right amount of a task, and how much reward should go into a contract.

"That book makes a lot of sense, Lynn," her father said. "When a job, or task, is too big, you have to reward more often. And going all night without bothering the pets is a big task for Pam. She has to have a reward right away. It's like on Jeff's contract where I initial the Task Record part each day he cleans his room. Each mark is sort of a small reward. Jeff knows if he has enough of them on Saturday, he can have his special time."

"But we can't be reading her a story every five or ten minutes. There wouldn't be time for anything else," Jeff said.

"No, you're right," Lynn agreed. "But we can change her contract so she gets one story after supper and another one before she goes to bed. Then she only has to be good to Rags and the fish for half of the evening each time."

"But even an hour might be too long the way Pamela acts," her mother said.

"I know. But there's another reward we can all give during the evening to help her make her contract," Lynn said. "We saw how she was creeping

closer and closer to the fish bowl and watching us all the time. But we ignored her. Finally, she couldn't stand it any more."

"I think you might be right," her father agreed. "If she'll act up to get our attention, she just might be good to get it too. It's worth a try."

"Okay, everybody," Lynn announced, "from now on when any of us sees that Pam isn't bothering the fish we'll just tell her what a big girl she is and how proud we are of her. And that goes for when she's playing nicely with Rags too. Everyone likes a lot of praise."

"And with all four of us helping, I just know she'll make her contract," Jeff said.

And the next night she did make her contract. And nearly every night after that.

NOW IT'S YOUR TURN, 7
MOM AND DAD

The whole Galen family gathered around the dining room table. They had planned to have a meeting each week to talk about everyone's contracts. Jeff's mother spoke first.

"You know, a few weeks ago I never would have thought we could all get along this well. Not only has everyone been doing their chores, but we've all been much nicer to each other, too. Like you, Jeff. Your room is almost always neat, and your dad says you've been much quieter in the afternoon when he's asleep."

Jeff's dad gave him a big wink.

"Of course," she went on, "we still have a fight or two. But for the most part, we're really getting along together."

"Even Pamela has been getting along with the pets," her husband added. "The fish don't hide behind the rocks anymore when she gets near the bowl!"

Lynn spoke up thoughtfully, "I think maybe our problem was that we all shouted at each other instead of really talking and listening."

"Right," her parents agreed.

"But still, some things are bothering Jeff and me. We've felt sort of funny about bringing them up though," Lynn said.

"Like what?" her father asked.

"Well, you and mom are always bugging us to do the things on our contracts. I think Jeff and I have shown that we're responsible enough to do those things most of the time without being reminded so much. And all that nagging just makes us both angry. Well, what I'm really saying is that Jeff and I want to do a contract with you two."

"With *us*!?" her parents asked, surprised.

"Yes, if you really want to be fair, you should be willing to make some changes for the better too. We'll even think up a special reward we can do for you if the contract works. What do you say?"

"Joe, she's got a good point at that!" her mother admitted. "You know kids, we don't mean to nag you. I guess we're just used to doing it, because we always had to remind you about everything before."

"So it's okay if Jeff and I draw up a contract for you?"

"Yes. Why not? It's a good idea."

"I'll get a blank contract." Jeff came back in a minute with one of the forms from Lynn's contracting book. The Galens had discovered it was much easier to write all of their contracts on the same form.

Lynn took the blank contract from her brother and began filling it in. She wrote "Mom and Dad" on the Task side and named the task "No nagging the kids." Then she wrote down some of the things they would count as nagging.

"Now," Lynn went on, "Jeff and I will mark each time you nag us."

"Yeah, and since you nag us so much now, we thought no nagging would be too hard for you at the start," Jeff added. "So we'll give each of you two a week. If you can go seven days without nagging us more than twice, you get your reward. Does that sound fair?"

"That part sounds okay. Now what about the other side of the contract?" Joseph Galen said. "We have to agree on a reward."

"We've talked about a good reward for you guys. We thought that making a whole dinner, cleaning up afterward, and taking care of Pam that night might be good," Lynn said. "Then you could go to a movie, or bowling, or do something else without worrying about us."

"You kids are terrific! Where do we sign?"

The Galens filled out the rest of the contract and everyone signed it.

"Now, I'll tape it on the refrigerator door," Jeff said. "All you have to do is look at the Task Record part of the contract, and you'll be able to see how much you're nagging us."

* * *

Two weeks later, Jeff and Lynn were peeling and slicing potatoes for the evening meal. "Hey, mom and dad really kept up their part of the contract, didn't they Lynn?"

"Yup. They're pretty super parents when you come right down to it. Lots of parents might not even listen to a far-out idea like contracts, but they gave it a try. For a while there it didn't look like they'd ever make

CONTRACT

TASK	REWARD

TASK

Who: *Mom and Dad*

What: *No nagging the kids*

When: *Every day*

How Well: *No more than 2 nags by mom and dad together for 7 days. Nag-ging is talking Jeff and Lynn to do the things on their contracts.*

REWARD

Who: *Lynn and Jeff*

What: *Cook supper and babysit night so mom and dad's*

When: *choose; after they make contract*

How Much: *Lynn and Jeff will pre-pare a whole dinner, clean up after-ward, and take care of Pamela so mom and dad can go out.*

Sign Here: *Lynn Stalen (Jeffrey Stalen)* Date: *April 22*

Sign Here: *Evelyn Stalen* Date: *April 22*
Joseph J. Stalen

TASK RECORD

	m	t	w	th	f	s	su	m	t	w	th	f	s	su	m
nags	0	2	1	0	2	0	0	0	0	1	0	0			
days	2	3	4	5	6 opt!	1	2	3	4	5	6 yes!				

their contract. They kept right on nagging as usual."

"I know," Jeff agreed. "But after they saw us marking down those nags on the contract, they really tried hard. It took them two weeks, but they made it. Boy, it's been great around here lately, hasn't it, Lynn?"

"Sure has. And the neatest thing is that mom and dad put us in control of our own contracts. We just check off when we do the task and then get our own rewards. Makes me feel more grown up and independent."

"It's even fun to help fix supper," Jeff said. "I never thought it would be. Just looked like a lot of work to me. Now I feel like a magician's helper, mixing a secret potion and presto!! — out comes the food all ready to eat!"

"It's not as easy as that, Jeff. There are lots of things about cooking that take time to learn."

"Would you teach me how to cook, Lynn?"

"Maybe sometime."

THE NUMBER PROBLEM 8

"I haven't seen Jeff since he got home from school over an hour ago," Lynn said. She was pouring milk into five glasses spaced around the dining room table.

"Now that you mention it, neither have I," her mother added. "He's usually the first one at the dinner table." Mom pulled a juicy roast from the oven and carried it into the dining room. "This ought to bring him running," she thought.

Joseph Galen finished mashing the potatoes and offered to get his son. "He probably started one of those paintings of his and doesn't even know what time it is."

But Jeff wasn't working on a painting. Instead, his dad found him sitting on the edge of his bed, looking very sad.

"Supper's almost ready, Jeffrey," his father said. But Jeff didn't move. He just kept staring at the floor. Joseph Galen sat on the bed next to his son and put his arm around him. "It's pretty clear something's bothering you, Jeff. Want to talk about it?"

"Oh, it's just that dumb old arithmetic again, dad. I just can't get good grades in it."

"Another test today, huh? I should have guessed it."

"I can't understand it, dad. I do okay in all my other subjects, but numbers and I just don't get along."

"Your mother and I are proud of your school work, Jeff. That's why we haven't said anything to you about your low arithmetic grades. You've done so well in everything else, we figured that grade would get better pretty soon."

"But it hasn't, dad. And I want to do better. Perry gets all 'A's' and he says he doesn't even have to study."

"Maybe arithmetic's easy for Perry. The way drawing pictures is for you . . ."

"Dad," Jeff interrupted, his face brightened. "Do you think a contract would work for this? Could we make a contract about my arithmetic?"

"Well," his father said, "we've had pretty good luck with our other contracts after we've gotten the bugs out of them. I'm willing to give it a try if you are. What do you say we go have supper and see what the rest of the family thinks about your idea?"

When Jeff mentioned his idea for a contract, Lynn spoke first. "But Jeff, a contract is an agreement between two or more people. How can you have a contract with yourself?"

"You're right, Lynn. Guess I'll have to forget it. But I'd do anything to get a better grade."

"Wait," Jeff's mother said. "I've got an idea that might help. Your arithmetic contract is something you want to do because you have a goal you want to reach. Right?"

"Right mom, I want to do better. I want to get a better grade."

"You could sign a contract with yourself," his mother went on, "and dad and I would help you stick to it. Then your contract would be more likely to help you reach your goal."

"But what could I do for my part of the contract? How do I

CONTRACT

TASK

Who: Jeff

What: Study arithmatic

When: Every school night

How Well: 1 hour studying arithmatic before any TV. Mom or dad
will time studying to make sure I
study for 1 hour every night.

REWARD

Who: Jeff

What: TV watching for Jeff
School nights after

When: completing task

How Much: As much TV as
Jeff wants before his badtime.

↑ Sign Here: _Jeffrey Golen_   Date: May 12

↑ Sign Here: _Jeffrey Golen_   Date: May 12

TASK RECORD

get better grades?''

"Now Jeff," his father said, "you can answer that question yourself. Just saying you want better grades won't do it. It will take lots of hard work and study."

"I study now. But it doesn't do any good."

"Oh, you always say you're going to study," his mother answered. "But how often do you *really* study your arithmetic? You always finish your homework in your favorite subjects first. Then there always seems to be a TV show you want to watch, and you never touch your arithmetic."

"But I like to watch TV, mom."

"That's it!" Lynn shouted.

"What's it?" everyone asked.

"Jeffrey's arithmetic contract, that's what," Lynn smiled. "If he wants to watch TV each night, Jeff would have to study arithmetic for a certain amount of time. That's pretty simple, isn't it?"

"Yeah, simple all right, but not very much fun," Jeff moaned.

"Well Jeff," his father said, "*you* were the one who wanted the better grade. If you don't want to give up something for . . ."

Jeff looked around the table. Everyone was watching him. Even little Pamela was looking at him with her big green eyes. He held up his hands to his father.

"Okay dad. You're right. I'll do whatever I have to to get an 'A'. Now, what's this contract going to look like?"

After supper Jeff sat down at the table with his parents to work out his new contract. They all agreed that before he could watch any TV on a school night, he'd have to spend an hour studying arithmetic. Jeff signed both the Task and the Reward side of the contract. He had made a contract with himself. His parents agreed to time his study hour each night to help him make his contract.

Jeff left the table and headed for his bedroom. He was going to start on his new contract right away. Besides, there was a good TV program he wanted to watch and it started in just one hour.

"Wait son," his father called to him.

Jeff stopped and walked back into the dining room.

"Your mother and I have been talking and we're very proud of you. It isn't every young man your age who decides by himself to do what you're doing. If you're willing to give up something you like to improve your grade, we want to do something to help you.

"Jeff, you've been getting 'C's' and 'D's' in arithmetic. This contract is supposed to help you improve your grade. We want it to work, so we'll set a goal you can reach now. After you've gotten a 'B', then we'll shoot for the 'A'."

"We think this project deserves two contracts, Jeffrey," his mother added.

Jeff watched his father take a new contract form and begin writing on it. "A super special surprise for Jeff if he gets a 'B' in arithmetic on his next report card."

"Wow, a surprise! Tell me what it is!"

CONTRACT

TASK

Who: _JEFF_

What: _GET A "B" IN ARITHMETIC._

When: _NEXT REPORT CARD_

How Well: _AT LEAST A "B"._

REWARD

Who: _MOM AND DAD_

What: _SPECIAL SURPRISE._ _AFTER JEFF COMPLETES_

When: _TASK_

How Much: _A SUPER SPECIAL SUR-_ _PRISE FOR JEFF IF HE GETS A "B" IN_ _ARITHMETIC ON HIS NEXT REPORT_ _CARD ._

Sign Here: _Jeffrey Galen_   Date: _May 12_

Sign Here: _Evelyn Galen_ _Joseph Jr. Galen_   Date: _May 12_

IN THIS FAMILY WE TRUST

G

TASK RECORD

"Why, if we told you now, it wouldn't be a surprise," his mother said. "We're sure you'll like it. That is, if you earn it."

* * *

Jeff worked hard on his new contract for the next two weeks. He got pretty angry at his parents one night when they wouldn't let him watch a special show he wanted to see. He had only studied for half an hour, and his parents made him miss half of the program while he spent another half hour with his homework.

At first Jeffrey couldn't understand why his parents were being so strict. After all, he did promise he'd finish his studying right after the show. But his parents made him stick to his contract. And besides, they said he could have finished his work earlier when he was painting. Then he wouldn't have had to miss any of the program.

When he thought about it later, Jeff had to admit his parents were right. They were only trying to help him keep his contract with himself. And once he started making excuses and getting away with watching TV before

studying, he knew his contract would break down. Pretty soon he wouldn't be studying at all, just like before.

But the contract still wasn't working, even though he followed it and did just what it said. He showed his parents his arithmetic papers from school. At the top of each paper was his usual grade, "C." Jeff was sad and confused. He'd done everything he could, but his grade hadn't improved.

"Maybe your teacher could help you," his mother suggested.

"I talked to her already," he said. "She said I'd have to do a lot better to get a 'B' on my next report card. I've been studying as hard as I can. It looks like I'm just wasting my time. I'm not smart enough to get a 'B' in arithmetic."

"I don't think that's the reason. Maybe your father and I haven't helped you on this the way we should have. We've all thought that just sending you to your room with your book for an hour each night would help your grade. The contract has worked all right. You *have* been spending an hour each night with your arithmetic book. But *time* spent with your books isn't what we want to change. We want you to *do* better in arithmetic. Let's try another approach. What do you say we write up a new contract?"

"We have to try something, mom. There are just three more weeks before report cards, and I want to earn that surprise. But what will the new contract say?"

"Okay, here's what we'll do. Each night after supper, your dad or I will give you 15 problems. They'll be just like the ones you're working on in school. The ones that have been giving you the most trouble. When you've gotten all of them right, you can watch TV, or do whatever else you like. And we'll help explain the extra hard ones to you."

"I think I like this way a lot better," Jeff said.

"Now your contract depends on solving problems, and that's how your grade will get better," his dad said. "Now *time* isn't the most important thing, but *doing* arithmetic problems is. Sometimes it will take you longer than an hour to do the new problems, sometimes less. But we'll all know you've learned to do 15 new problems each day."

CONTRACT

TASK

Who: Jeff

What: Solving arithmetic problems. Each school night

When: after supper

How Well: Jeff must solve 15 problems. Dad or mom will assign problems like the ones Jeff has trouble with in school. Mom and dad will check Jeff's work and explain hard ones to him.

REWARD

Who: Jeff

What: TV watching for Jeff School nights

When: completing task after

How Much: As much TV as Jeff wants before his bedtime.

Sign Here: *Jeffrey Halen*   Date: May 26

Sign Here: *Jeffrey Halen*   Date: May 26

TASK RECORD

Jeff knew just what he had to do each night — figure out those problems — and as soon as he got them done, he could watch TV. That sure was better than before, when he would spend a lot of his study time daydreaming and just hoping the hour would be over.

Jeff went to bed that night and dreamed about what his surprise might be.

WHAT'S COOKING   9

Jeff enjoyed the walk home from school most of the time. He loved to look into the shops as he passed. The bakery window was heaped with fresh rolls, cakes, and cookies. The butcher shop had barbecued chickens that made his mouth water. And the fruits and vegetables looked shiny and juicy in the supermarket window. But the toys and models in the hobby store were his favorite.

Today though, Jeff didn't stop to look. Instead he walked straight home very quickly. He knew his grades would be in the mail, and he hoped his arithmetic grade would be better. After all, he'd worked much harder since he changed his homework contract. Jeff wondered what the special surprise would be if he got a "B." His parents would probably tell him the news after dinner at the family meeting.

He heard a radio playing and his sister singing as he came into the house. Lynn stopped and looked up as her brother entered the kitchen.

"What's for supper, Lynn?"

"Meat loaf, home fried potatoes, and green beans."

"That should be fun to make. Can I help?"

"Thanks Jeff, but it would just take me much longer if I had to show you how to do everything. And I want to start dinner as fast as I can, because I'm working on a big project in my room."

"What project?"

"I decided to paint my bedroom furniture again. It's so old and scratched up. It looks awful. So I got a book on refinishing furniture from the school library and bought some sandpaper and paint with my babysitting money. Anyhow, it takes a long time to do a good job, so I need all the time I can get."

"Say, Lynn, I have an idea."

"By the gleam in your eye, I can tell you're up to something, little brother."

"Well, you never said anything about kids having contracts with each other. Why don't *we* work one out?"

"I had a feeling you were thinking about something like that. Well, why

CONTRACT

TASK

Who: Lynn

What: Cooking lesson for Jeff

When: When Lynn is fixing supper

How Well: Lynn will let Jeff try
to do everything and tell him all
about recipes and measurements.

▲ Sign Here: *Lynn Halen*

▲ Sign Here: *Jeffrey Halen*

REWARD

Who: Jeff

What: Help Lynn with her
furniture

When: Nights that Jeff gets a
cooking lesson.

How Much: Jeff will help Lynn
sand and paint her bedroom
furniture for one half hour.

Date: June 16

Date: June 16

IN THIS FAMILY WE TRUST
G ★

TASK RECORD

not? How about if I give you a cooking lesson while I'm making dinner, then you help me sand and paint my furniture that night for half an hour? That would be a fair trade, wouldn't it?"

"Would you let me try to do everything and explain about recipes and measuring and things?"

"Sure."

"Then it's a deal!" he shouted, and Lynn and Jeff shook hands. "I'll get a contract form and we'll write it up."

* * *

"The Galen family meeting will now begin," Jeff's mother said.

"It won't be long now," he thought.

"Things have been really good around here the last few weeks," his father said. And everyone, including Pam, nodded yes. "Lynn's been doing her chores like clockwork, and Jeff's room looks good all the time. In fact, I'm wondering if we need to keep up those two contracts any longer. Of course, we'd still expect you to do your chores and you'd still get your

rewards, but we would only check once in a while. Just to be sure everything's okay. You've shown us how much we can trust you."

"Thanks dad," Jeff and Lynn said together.

"Pamela's contract has worked really well so far too, but I think we should go on with it for a while," Joseph Galen went on. "She's pretty young and she might forget."

"Mom, dad, what about my homework contract? Did the grades come?" Jeff asked. He couldn't wait any longer.

"Yes, dear. Here, see for yourself."

Jeff tore open the report card and saw his arithmetic grade.

"It's a 'B'! *Hooray!*"

"Congratulations!" Lynn said.

Pam clapped her hands.

"Your mother and I are proud of you, Jeff. And I bet you're wondering about the surprise we have in store for you. Let's see, I think the surprise will have to wait until tomorrow if it's okay with you. Why don't you ask

Perry to come with us on our weekly outing. We'll have the surprise then."

"Sure dad," Jeff said. He was getting more and more excited.

* * *

At noon on Saturday, Jeff was all set to go with his father for their outing. Perry arrived with his model plane tucked under his arm. And the three of them climbed into the car and drove off toward the park. Jeff was a little disappointed. He did love to fly Perry's airplane, but going to the park was not the surprise he'd expected. He'd been hoping his father would take them someplace special.

Jeff's dad stopped the car at the edge of the park. "C'mon you guys. Let's fly Perry's plane in the open field."

Perry and Jeff followed Joseph Galen across the field. "Oh, I forgot something in the trunk of the car. Jeff, would you get it for me?"

His father tossed the keys. Jeff caught them and headed for the car. What could his dad have forgotten? He opened the trunk and just stared at the open box in front of him. He was so surprised he didn't hear his father

and Perry come up behind him.

"It's just like mine, Jeff. Your dad even called my dad to find out where to buy one."

"Like it?" his father asked.

"Oh dad, it's beautiful! Thanks!"

Jeff carefully lifted the light blue model airplane from its wrappings. He knew this was going to be one of the best days of his life.

DO-IT-YOURSELF CONTRACTING KIT

THE _____
(your family's name)

DO-IT-YOURSELF CONTRACTING KIT

Here is a complete Contracting Kit to use in your own home. This kit will help your family set up contracts just like Lynn's book helped the Galen family set up theirs. It will help you:

1. Have a Family Meeting to start planning your contracts

2. Choose a Task

3. Choose a Reward

4. Write a Contract

5. Stick to the Rules for Successful Contracting

It's a good idea for the family to read the whole kit together first. Then go back to the first part and begin by having a Family Meeting.

Remember: After you start using contracts, look back at this kit whenever you need to. If you've started a contract and it's not working — *Change It!* The Rules section will help you find what may be wrong with your contract so you can fix it.

One last word before you start. Planning contracts can seem a bit hard at first, but the more you do, the easier it gets!

1. *The Family Meeting.* Holding a Family Meeting at the table after supper is a good way to start planning your contracts. The first meeting is the most important, so plan to spend one or two hours at it. *Don't Rush!* If you haven't finished all the sections in the kit during the first meeting, you should stop and pick up where you left off the next night.

You can run a Family Meeting in two ways. Some families, like the Galens, may decide to discuss their problems informally. If you decide to do it this way, give each person three to five minutes to talk without being interrupted. Give everyone a pencil and paper to use during the meeting. Be as *specific* as possible when you talk about things you or others do or don't do that you would like to see changed. In other words, say *exactly* what the person does or doesn't do. Read the following examples. They should give you some hints about being *specific*.

Say This:	*Not This:*
Marsha leaves her coat on the floor after school.	Marsha is lazy.
Scott helps put away the groceries and takes out the trash.	Scott is a nice boy.
Fran doesn't water the plants.	Fran doesn't cooperate.
Dad doesn't let me use his shop.	Dad is mean to me.

I leave my toys on the floor and stairs.	I'm sloppy.
John gets dressed by himself.	John is a big boy.

Remember: Write and say *exactly* what the person *does* or *doesn't do.* Be as *specific* as you can.

Here is a list of tasks family members often use. They may give you some good ideas for this step.

Examples of Tasks for Family Contracts

Following instructions	Feeding, washing, walking pets
Trying new foods	Doing grocery shopping
Dressing self	Taking phone messages correctly
Washing hands	Taking out trash
Washing dishes	Raking leaves
Cleaning room	Being a safe driver
Running errands	Doing physical exercises
Vacuuming	Playing quietly alone
Sweeping	Doing a task without being asked
Mowing lawn	Losing weight
Washing car	Polishing shoes
Babysitting for younger brother/sister	Helping younger brother/sister with a task
Brushing teeth	Putting away toys

Washing floors	Practicing musical instrument
Dusting furniture	Doing farm chores
Washing windows	Weeding garden
Doing homework	Keeping own savings account
Cleaning garage	Sharing toys with brother/sister
Setting table for dinner	Taking care of bike
Cooking	Having proper table manners
Doing laundry	Shoveling walks and driveway
Packing sandwiches for family	Hanging up coats
Making bed	Ironing
Cleaning basement	Painting
Defrosting and cleaning refrigerator	Removing ashes from furnace/fireplace
Bringing in wood for fireplace	Collecting newspapers for recycling
Returning soda bottles	Watering plants and shrubs
Folding clothes	Being on time for dinner

When everyone has finished talking, take a few minutes to talk about and write down some possible rewards. Each person should list several activities, special privileges, or treats they really enjoy.

Here is a list of rewards that family members often use. They may give you some good ideas for this step.

Examples of Rewards for Family Contracts

Wall decorations	Staying up late one night
Clothing	Playing pinball
Cooking	Going someplace by yourself
Fishing equipment	Science kits
Praise	Art, dancing, or other lessons
Money	Using the family car
Special food treats	Playing catch
Watching TV	Allowance
Models	Going to the library
Trips to zoo, parks, museums	Coloring book
Picnics	Dolls
Movies	Arts and crafts kits and supplies
Amusement park	Puzzles
Free time	Pets
Having a friend stay overnight	Camera
A party	Going swimming, skating, etc.
Inviting friends on trips	Books
Having stories read to you	Records
Special time alone with parent	Playing games — darts, chess, checkers, cards, Scrabble, etc.
Hobby materials	Camping
Horseback riding	Hiking

Staying out late one night	Toys
Sports equipment	Subscription to a magazine
Eating out	Making phone calls
Being given responsibility around house	Tickets to sporting events, plays, etc.
Bicycle	Blocks
Going to special school functions	Stamps, coins, rocks for collection

Another way to run the meeting is to have each family member fill out three lists. First, tear out copies of List A from the back of this kit and give one to each person. Take a few minutes to fill it out. *Remember again:* Be as *specific* as possible. On the left side of the form write down the things you already *do* to help your family. On the right side write down the things you *could do* to help. These are things you know you should be doing, but haven't been getting done lately. Or, maybe there's something you've never done before, but you'd like to start doing it for your family or yourself. Write it down. Maybe a contract can help.

After everyone has completed their own List A, put these lists aside and give each family member a copy of List B. Have each person write their name in the three blank spaces at the top. Now, pass each person's List B around the table slowly. Give everyone else in the family a chance to add to it. Everyone should write at least one thing on each side of everyone else's List B. *Remember:* Everyone writes on your List B, except you!

And now for the fun part! After everyone has filled out Lists A and B,

Here's a Copy of List A Filled Out by Fourteen-Year-Old Jean

List A   Name: Jean

THINGS I DO TO HELP MY FAMILY

OTHER WAYS I COULD HELP MY FAMILY AND MYSELF

1. Feed Queenie and Chippy
2. Clean up my bedroom
3. Practice my piano

4. Wash dishes

5. Help dad with the laundry
6.

7.

1. Be on time for supper
2. Turn off the lights when I leave a room
3. Dust the living room

4. Clean up the back yard
5. Hang up my coat when I get home from school
6.

7.

List A   Name: _Mom_

THINGS I DO TO HELP MY FAMILY

OTHER WAYS I COULD HELP MY FAMILY AND MYSELF

Things I do to help my family:

1. Cook supper

2. Drive Jean to parties, bowling, etc.

3. Go to work every day

4. Pay bills

5. Share housework with Phil — dusting, vacuuming, etc.

6.

7.

Other ways I could help my family and myself:

1. Teach Jean to play guitar

2. Spend less time on phone

3. Clean up the basement

4. Help Jean with her homework.

5. Help Phil in the garden

6.

7.

Here's an Example of List B Made for Eight-Year-Old Bobby

List B

Name: _Bobby_

THINGS _Bobby_ DOES
TO HELP THE FAMILY

1. _Vacuums when asked_
2. _Makes his bed_
3. _Reads stories to little sister_
4. _Empties trash_
5. _Rakes leaves_
6. _____
7. _____

OTHER WAYS _Bobby_
COULD HELP THE FAMILY

1. _Put his dirty clothes in hamper_
2. _Do homework at night without being asked_
3. _Make his own sandwiches for his school lunch_
4. _Clean and sponge off table after supper_
5. _____
6. _____
7. _____

give each person a copy of List C. Fill out List C with all the things you like to do best, the things you'd like to have and your favorite treats. You can discuss these ideas with the rest of your family. It's all right if two or more people put down the same rewards. The rewards you write down on List C can be everyday things you like to do. Or they can be special — something you've been wanting to do or wanting to have for a long time. Write down as many as you like. Use the back of the sheet if you need more room.

If you have young children in your family, like Pamela Galen, who don't write yet, you can talk with them about simple tasks. Then you can ask them to tell the family what their favorite things are. Someone else in the family can fill out the lists for a person who doesn't write.

When you've finished with List C, pass each person their other two lists. Now take a few minutes and have everybody read their own lists carefully. If somebody wrote something that you don't understand on your List B, *Ask*.

All finished? Good! Now you're ready to choose a task for your first contract.

2. *Choosing a Task*. This is the time for everyone to look at Lists A and B closely. Go around the table and try to help each person decide which task is the *most important* for them to start first. Ask the following questions to help each other decide which task to choose: Would this person be a better family member if they did this task? Would the family be happier and better off if they did this task regularly? Is this task something the person can do? Are they able to handle it?

Fourteen-Year-Old Sue Ann Filled Out Her List C Like This

List C Name: *Sue Ann*

MY FAVORITE THINGS, ACTIVITIES, AND SPECIAL TREATS

1. Listening to records
2. Movies
3. Playing pinball
4. Miniature golf
5. Swimming
6. Ice skating
7. Ice cream sundaes
8. Aquarium and fish
9. Picnics
10. Coin collection
11. Riding a horse
12. Fishing with dad
13.
14.
15.

List C
Name: DAD

MY FAVORITE THINGS, ACTIVITIES, AND SPECIAL TREATS

1. Bowling
2. Breakfast in bed
3. Books about gardening
4. Basketball games
5. Sitting in my chair with no one bothering me
6. Watching TV
7. Playing poker with my friends
8. Movies with the kids
9. Box seat ticket for a big league game
10. Going out to dinner with mom
11. Making homemade bread
12.
13.
14.
15.

If the answers to these questions are yes, you've probably chosen an important task. Remember too, contracts work best when all the people who sign them agree that the task is important.

Once each family member has chosen one task, write the task in very *specific* words. These words should tell exactly *what* the task is, and *how well* it has to be done. Remember how important it was for the Galens to be specific about Jeff's room cleaning contract? It didn't work until they wrote *exactly* what he had to do to clean his room. Here are some examples to give you hints about being specific:

Name of Task	*Task specifics*
Get ready for bed.	▪ Hands and face washed.
	Teeth brushed.
	Pajamas on.
	Clothes hung in closet or put in drawers.
Clean up yard.	▪ Put all papers in trash can.
	Put all toys and tools in garage.
Be nice to little brother.	▪ Play a game with him or read to him.
	Help him put away his toys.
	Don't hit him.
	Don't call him "dumb" or "stupid."

Pay more attention to my daughter.	Ask her about her homework.
	Ask her what she thinks about something.
	Praise her for something she did or is doing.
	Invite her to help me do something.

Once you've written the tasks this way, decide *when* or *how often* they must be done. Must they be completed every day, twice a week, on Saturdays, at a special time, or as often as the person wants to get the reward? Here are some examples:

Name of Task	*When (How Often)*
Get ready for bed.	▪ Sunday through Thursday by 9:30 p.m.
	Friday and Saturday by 10:30 p.m.
Clean up yard.	▪ Friday or Saturday each week.
Be nice to little brother.	▪ Play with him or read to him at least 30 minutes every day.
	Never hit him.
	Don't call him "dumb" or "stupid" more than once a week.

Pay more attention to my daughter.

- Do two of the following four task specifics at least once a day:

Ask her about her homework.

Ask her what she thinks about something.

Praise her for something she did or is doing.

Invite her to help me do something.

The last things to check are *exceptions* to the task. In the story, Jeff could miss one day every week on his room cleaning contract without losing his reward. Some tasks really must be done every day — tasks like feeding the cat, cooking supper for a hungry family, or doing your homework. But you might skip other tasks now and then without losing your reward — tasks like practicing your musical instrument, making your bed, or helping someone else in your family work on a special project. *Remember,* no one is perfect! So, if you're going to allow exceptions, write them into the contract! Then no one can argue about it later.

Let's move on to the fun part now!

3. *Choosing a Reward.* Now everyone should take List C and look at it closely. Go around the table and have each person pick a reward from their List C for doing the task they've chosen. It's very important that the reward is *fair* for everyone. The reward should be big enough to give you something to look forward to while you're doing the task, but it shouldn't be too big!

The following examples will give you some hints about being *fair:*

Task	Fair Reward	Unfair Reward
Doing homework every night	One hour of TV	Five minutes of TV
Taking out trash each day	Help dad bake cookies once a week	Maybe go to a movie next month
Practicing trumpet three times a week	Eat pizza out once every two weeks	Eat pizza out every night you practice

Ask yourself the following questions: Is the reward too small for the task? Is the reward too big for the task? If the answer to either of these questions is yes, go back and change the reward so that it's *fair. Remember:* Both people who sign the contract have to agree that the reward is fair! Not just one.

Be sure the reward is *specific* too. Write exactly *how much* reward you'll earn and *when* you'll get it. For example, Don and his parents agreed that if he did the dishes three times a week he could have one or two friends over for supper on Sunday night. This seemed *fair* to all of them.

Most of the time, you'll choose one reward for each task. But sometimes a person will want to list several rewards and then choose one. This is okay too. Don's sister Allison and her parents agreed on the following choice of rewards:

1. Go to the swimming pool with mom for two hours on Saturday or Sunday.

2. Go to a movie that she wanted to see after she did her task for two weeks.

3. $1.50 for each week she completed her task.

She could choose from this list if she babysat for her younger sister Laura Lee three afternoons a week.

Or, the reward may be very big, or special, like getting a record player, going out to dinner, or taking a trip to the zoo in a nearby city. These rewards are too big to be given every day or every week. But you can still use them in your contracts if you use a simple point system. This means every time you do the task, you'll earn a point. After you've earned a certain number of points, you can trade them in to get your reward. How many points is a reward worth? It depends on the reward and what the task is. But remember, it must be a number that both people who sign the contract agree on. It must be *fair*. And just like everything else with contracts, you must *write it* on the contract. That way no one will argue later about how many points the reward was worth.

Here's a list of rewards and the points that the Moyer family needed to get each reward.

Rewards	Point Value
Ice cream soda or malt	5
45 rpm record	8
Go to movies	15

Set of paints	25
Model	25
Subscription to magazine	40
Tickets to the circus	50
Set of stamps for collection	60
Ping pong table	300

By now everyone in your family should have chosen a task and a reward. It's time to write the contracts!

4. *Writing a Contract.* Contracts should look nice and be easy to read. They should have all the information about the task and reward you've decided on and written down in the last two steps. We've included some tear-out contract forms in the kit for you to use. They are just like the ones the Galens used. Or, you can draw up a contract form of your own if you like. If you use the contract forms included with this kit, you can design your own family seal just like Jeff did for the Galens. Put your own seal on the bottom right hand corner of the contract. That makes it look official!

Tear out one of the contract forms and look at it carefully. On the left side of the contract you'll find space to fill in the name of the person *Who* will be doing the task and getting the reward. After you fill it in, write *What* the name of the task is. Then write *When* the task is to be done. Every day. Twice a week. Once a week. Before going to school each day, and so forth. After *How Well*, fill in the task specifics. Be sure to write down exactly what the person must do to complete the task. If you're going to allow exceptions, write them in here.

On the right side of the contract fill in *Who* will be giving the reward, *What* it will be, *When* it will be given, and *How Much* reward will be given.

Both people — the task person and the reward person — should now sign their names to the contract in the *Sign Here* spaces. Also, write down the date. This will help you remember how long each contract has been set up.

Notice the section at the bottom of the contract called the *Task Record.* You can use the *Task Record* to keep track of doing the task and getting the reward. If you like, you can fill in which days you're supposed to do the task, then check off the day each time you complete the task. If you're using a point system, you can use the *Task Record* to mark down the number of points you've earned. Look back at the contracts the Galens wrote and see how they used the *Task Record.*

Remember: You can still make a contract with someone even if they don't read or write. Remember Jeff's idea for Pamela's contract? You can always draw or cut out and paste on pictures to stand for the task and the reward. Set up the contract the same way, just use pictures instead of words.

On the next two pages are contracts the Cooper family started. Look at them carefully. They are good examples of well-written contracts.

Sometimes it's a good idea to use the contract itself to remind everyone. The Galens taped Pamela's contract right to the fish bowl. Lynn reminded herself to get supper started each night by hanging her contract on a kitchen

CONTRACT

TASK

Who: Mary Ellen

What: Clean up garage

When: 1st Sat. of each month

How Well: 1. Sweep floor 2. Put tools away 3. Hang up all garden equipment

Sign Here: ▲ Mary Cooper   Date: 7/21

Sign Here: ▲ Sandy Cooper   Date: July 21

REWARD

Cooper Family Seal

Who: Sandy

What: Wash, clean Mary Ellen's car

When: 1st Sat. of each month

How Much: 1. Wash and rinse outside 2. Vacuum floor 3. Wash windows

TASK RECORD

	Aug	Sept	Oct	Nov	Dec	Jan	Feb	Mar	Apr	May	June	July	Aug	Sept	Oct
Garg.	X	X	X	X	X	X	X								
Car	X	X	X	X	X	X	X								

CONTRACT

TASK	REWARD
Who: Ben	**Who:** Mary Ellen
What: Pack sandwiches for whole family	**What:** Cook Ben's favorite meal
When: Every day: Mon.-Fri. by 8 a.m.	**When:** Once each week: Sat. or Sun.
How Well: 1 sandwich for each person, packed in bag with napkin.	**How Much:** Anything Ben wants for supper as long as it doesn't cost more than $5.00.
Exception – only if Ben is sick.	

Sign Here: Ben Cooper   Date: July 30

Sign Here: Mary Ellen Cooper   Date: 30 July

Cooper Family Seals

TASK RECORD

m	t	w	th	f	m	t	w	th	f	m	t	w	th	f
X	X	X	X	X	X	X	X	X	X	X	X	X	sick	X
X	X	X	X	X	X	X	X	X	X	X	X	X	X	

cabinet door. If you made a contract with yourself to do your homework like Jeff did, where would be a good place to hang it? Right! A good place would be right in front of your desk or the place you study each night. If you don't hang up your contract to remind yourself, put it in a safe but handy place so you can look at it whenever you need to.

Now your contract is ready to go! Good work! Good luck!

5. *Rules for Successful Contracting.* It's a good idea to check through the following Rules *before* you start your contract. You'll have a much better chance to have it work if you try to work out all the problems first.

Now sometimes you'll miss something and your contract won't go the way you planned. This happened several times to the Galens. But they always tried again. So, if your contract doesn't work out the first time, *TRY AGAIN!* Go back and check the Rules. You'll probably see what's wrong with your contract. Then you can change it and get a new start!

Rule 1. The contract should be *written.* Don't trust your memory. If you write the whole contract and keep it in a handy place, you can look back at it whenever you have any questions.

Rule 2. The contract must be *specific.* Check to see that you have included all of the following information in your contract:

———— Task   ———— Who

———— What

———— When

———— How Well

———— Exceptions (if any)

_____ Reward   _____ Who

                                         _____ What

                                         _____ When

                                         _____ How Much

Then ask these questions:

_____ Does everyone understand the contract?

_____ Is the task the right size? Can the person do it?

_____ Is the reward the right size?

Rule 3. The contract should be _positive._ The contract should say that doing a task earns a reward. This way you don't need to use threats. Just follow the signed agreement. If the task is done, the person gets the reward. If the task is not done, the person doesn't get the reward.

Rule 4. The contract must be _fair._ You learned from the story that a contract is an agreement that you will get a reward for doing a certain task. This agreement will help your family work together better if everyone agrees that both the task and the reward are fair.

Rule 5. The reward should be _immediate._ Each person should be able to have the reward as soon as the task is finished. If you're on a point system, you should get a check mark on the _Task Record_ as soon as you finish the task.

Rule 6. The contract must be _honest._ Don't promise a reward you really can't give. This causes bad feelings because it isn't honest. Choose a reward that can be given _every time_ it's earned. The same goes for the task.

Don't sign a contract that calls for a task you know you can't do. Be reasonable on both sides. *Remember:* If you don't do the task, you won't get the reward.

Rule 7. You should *change the contract* whenever you need to. Don't be afraid to change a contract that doesn't work. We all make mistakes! Just be sure that both people agree on all the changes, then try again. And good luck this time!

TEAR-OUT CONTRACTING FORMS

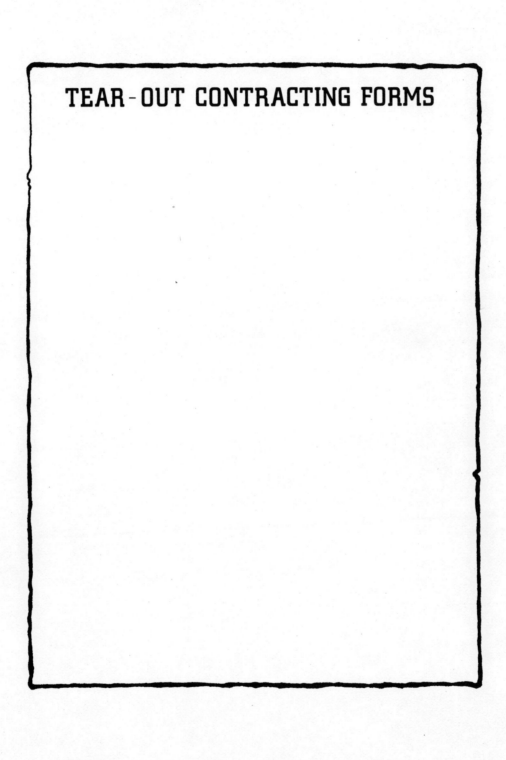

List A

Name: _____

THINGS I DO TO HELP MY FAMILY	OTHER WAYS I COULD HELP MY FAMILY AND MYSELF
1. _____	1. _____
_____	_____
2. _____	2. _____
_____	_____
3. _____	3. _____
_____	_____
4. _____	4. _____
_____	_____
5. _____	5. _____
_____	_____
6. _____	6. _____
_____	_____
7. _____	7. _____
_____	_____

List A

Name: _____

THINGS I DO TO HELP MY FAMILY

OTHER WAYS I COULD HELP MY FAMILY AND MYSELF

1. _____ _____	1. _____ _____
2. _____ _____	2. _____ _____
3. _____ _____	3. _____ _____
4. _____ _____	4. _____ _____
5. _____ _____	5. _____ _____
6. _____ _____	6. _____ _____
7. _____ _____	7. _____ _____

List A

Name: _____

THINGS I DO TO HELP MY FAMILY

OTHER WAYS I COULD HELP MY FAMILY AND MYSELF

1. _____

_____

2. _____

_____

3. _____

_____

4. _____

_____

5. _____

_____

6. _____

_____

7. _____

_____

1. _____

_____

2. _____

_____

3. _____

_____

4. _____

_____

5. _____

_____

6. _____

_____

7. _____

_____

List A

Name: _____

THINGS I DO TO HELP MY FAMILY	OTHER WAYS I COULD HELP MY FAMILY AND MYSELF
1. _____ _____	1. _____ _____
2. _____ _____	2. _____ _____
3. _____ _____	3. _____ _____
4. _____ _____	4. _____ _____
5. _____ _____	5. _____ _____
6. _____ _____	6. _____ _____
7. _____ _____	7. _____ _____

List A

Name: _____

THINGS I DO TO HELP MY FAMILY

OTHER WAYS I COULD HELP MY FAMILY AND MYSELF

1. _____
_____

2. _____
_____

3. _____
_____

4. _____
_____

5. _____
_____

6. _____
_____

7. _____
_____

1. _____
_____

2. _____
_____

3. _____
_____

4. _____
_____

5. _____
_____

6. _____
_____

7. _____
_____

List B

Name: _____

THINGS _____ DOES
TO HELP THE FAMILY

OTHER WAYS _____
COULD HELP THE FAMILY

1. _____
_____

2. _____
_____

3. _____
_____

4. _____
_____

5. _____
_____

6. _____
_____

7. _____
_____

1. _____
_____

2. _____
_____

3. _____
_____

4. _____
_____

5. _____
_____

6. _____
_____

7. _____
_____

List B

Name: _____

THINGS _____ DOES
TO HELP THE FAMILY

OTHER WAYS _____
COULD HELP THE FAMILY

1. _____

_____

2. _____

_____

3. _____

_____

4. _____

_____

5. _____

_____

6. _____

_____

7. _____

_____

1. _____

_____

2. _____

_____

3. _____

_____

4. _____

_____

5. _____

_____

6. _____

_____

7. _____

_____

List B

Name: _____

THINGS _____ DOES
TO HELP THE FAMILY

1. _____
   _____
2. _____
   _____
3. _____
   _____
4. _____
   _____
5. _____
   _____
6. _____
   _____
7. _____
   _____

OTHER WAYS _____
COULD HELP THE FAMILY

1. _____
   _____
2. _____
   _____
3. _____
   _____
4. _____
   _____
5. _____
   _____
6. _____
   _____
7. _____
   _____

List B

Name: _____

THINGS _____ DOES
TO HELP THE FAMILY

OTHER WAYS _____
COULD HELP THE FAMILY

1. _____

_____

2. _____

_____

3. _____

_____

4. _____

_____

5. _____

_____

6. _____

_____

7. _____

_____

1. _____

_____

2. _____

_____

3. _____

_____

4. _____

_____

5. _____

_____

6. _____

_____

7. _____

_____

List B

Name: _____

THINGS _____ DOES
TO HELP THE FAMILY

1. _____

_____

2. _____

_____

3. _____

_____

4. _____

_____

5. _____

_____

6. _____

_____

7. _____

_____

OTHER WAYS _____
COULD HELP THE FAMILY

1. _____

_____

2. _____

_____

3. _____

_____

4. _____

_____

5. _____

_____

6. _____

_____

7. _____

_____

List C

Name:_____

MY FAVORITE THINGS, ACTIVITIES, AND SPECIAL TREATS

1._____
2._____
3._____
4._____
5._____
6._____
7._____
8._____
9._____
10._____
11._____
12._____
13._____
14._____
15._____

List C

Name:_____

MY FAVORITE THINGS, ACTIVITIES, AND SPECIAL TREATS

1._____

2._____

3._____

4._____

5._____

6._____

7._____

8._____

9._____

10._____

11._____

12._____

13._____

14._____

15._____

List C

Name:_____

MY FAVORITE THINGS, ACTIVITIES, AND SPECIAL TREATS

1._____

2._____

3._____

4._____

5._____

6._____

7._____

8._____

9._____

10._____

11._____

12._____

13._____

14._____

15._____

List C

Name:_____

MY FAVORITE THINGS, ACTIVITIES, AND SPECIAL TREATS

1._____
2._____
3._____
4._____
5._____
6._____
7._____
8._____
9._____
10._____
11._____
12._____
13._____
14._____
15._____

List C

Name:_____

MY FAVORITE THINGS, ACTIVITIES, AND SPECIAL TREATS

1. _____

2. _____

3. _____

4. _____

5. _____

6. _____

7. _____

8. _____

9. _____

10. _____

11. _____

12. _____

13. _____

14. _____

15. _____

CONTRACT

TASK

Who: _____

What: _____

When: _____

How Well: _____

_____

_____

REWARD

Who: _____

What: _____

When: _____

How Much: _____

_____

_____

➤ Sign Here: _____ Date: _____

➤ Sign Here: _____ Date: _____

TASK RECORD

CONTRACT

TASK

Who: _____

What: _____

When: _____

How Well: _____

REWARD

Who: _____

What: _____

When: _____

How Much: _____

Sign Here: _____ Date: _____

Sign Here: _____ Date: _____

TASK RECORD

CONTRACT

TASK

Who: _____

What: _____

When: _____

How Well: _____

REWARD

Who: _____

What: _____

When: _____

How Much: _____

Sign Here: _____ Date: _____

Sign Here: _____ Date: _____

TASK RECORD

CONTRACT

TASK

Who: _____

What: _____

When: _____

How Well: _____

_____

_____

REWARD

Who: _____

What: _____

When: _____

How Much: _____

_____

_____

▼ Sign Here: _____ Date: _____

▼ Sign Here: _____ Date: _____

TASK RECORD

CONTRACT

TASK

Who: _____

What: _____

When: _____

How Well: _____

_____

_____

REWARD

Who: _____

What: _____

When: _____

How Much: _____

_____

_____

▼ Sign Here: _____ Date: _____

▼ Sign Here: _____ Date: _____

TASK RECORD

CONTRACT

TASK

Who: _____

What: _____

When: _____

How Well: _____

_____

_____

_____

_____

REWARD

Who: _____

What: _____

When: _____

How Much: _____

_____

_____

_____

_____

▼ Sign Here: _____ Date: _____

▼ Sign Here: _____ Date: _____

TASK RECORD

CONTRACT

TASK

Who: _____

What: _____

When: _____

How Well: _____

REWARD

Who: _____

What: _____

When: _____

How Much: _____

Sign Here: _____ Date: _____

Sign Here: _____ Date: _____

TASK RECORD

CONTRACT

TASK | REWARD

Who: _____

What: _____

When: _____

How Well: _____

Who: _____

What: _____

When: _____

How Much: _____

Sign Here: _____ Date: _____

Sign Here: _____ Date: _____

TASK RECORD

CONTRACT

TASK

Who: _____

What: _____

When: _____

How Well: _____

_____

_____

_____

REWARD

Who: _____

What: _____

When: _____

How Much: _____

_____

_____

_____

Sign Here: _____ Date: _____

Sign Here: _____ Date: _____

TASK RECORD
